Gooseberry Patch

RV cooking

Classics

Far away is only far away if you don't
go there.
-Unknown

★ Classics ★

Omelets in a Bag

2 eggs
cooked sausage
chopped ham
shredded cheeses
chopped onion

chopped green pepper
chopped tomato
chopped mushrooms
salsa

Have each guest write his or her name with permanent pen on a quart-size plastic zipping freezer bag. Place 2 eggs in bag and shake to scramble. Add other ingredients to bag as desired. Press the air out of bag and zip it up. Bring a large pot of water to a rolling boil; place up to 6 or 8 bags at a time into pot. (Use a large pot so freezer bags float freely and don't touch sides of pot.) Boil bags for 13 to 15 minutes. When done, open bags and omelets will roll out easily. Make as many as needed.

Get together with new friends in camp for an Omelets in a Bag party! Whether you're cooking indoors at your RV's stove or outdoors over a campfire, you'll be sharing laughs along with good food.

Brown Sugar Muffins

1/2 c. butter
1 c. brown sugar, packed
1 egg
2 c. all-purpose flour

1 t. baking soda
1/4 t. salt
1 c. milk
1 t. vanilla extract

Mix together butter and brown sugar; add egg and blend thoroughly. Add flour, baking soda and salt; mix. Add milk and vanilla; stir until moistened. Spray muffin tin with non-stick vegetable spray; fill muffin cups 2/3 full. Bake at 375 degrees for 15 to 20 minutes. Makes one dozen.

If you love freshly baked muffins, pack a set of stackable, reusable silicone baking cups. They're easy to store and oh-so handy for other uses like serving mini portions of chips, nuts or fruit.

Midwestern Shredded Chicken Sandwiches

1 T. butter	1 T. cornstarch
1 onion, diced	1/2 c. milk
1 stalk celery, chopped	salt and pepper to taste
1 c. chicken broth, divided	6 sandwich buns, split
3 boneless, skinless	
chicken breasts	

Melt butter in a large saucepan; sauté onion, celery and one tablespoon broth for 5 minutes. Add chicken and remaining broth; bring to a boil. Reduce heat; simmer until chicken is tender, about 15 to 20 minutes. Remove chicken from saucepan and allow to cool, reserving broth. Shred chicken; return to broth in saucepan and bring to a simmer. Whisk cornstarch and milk together in a small bowl; slowly stir into chicken mixture. Simmer and stir until mixture is thickened but still moist, about 8 minutes. Add salt and pepper to taste; spoon onto buns. Makes 6 sandwiches.

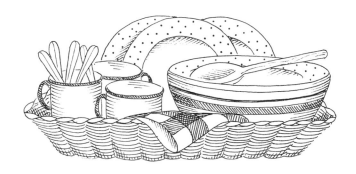

On your first night out, sit down to a homemade freezer meal...just heat & eat! Prepare favorite foods at home and freeze portions flat in plastic zipping bags...easy to stack, quick to thaw.

Waldorf Salad

1/2 c. mayonnaise
2 T. orange juice
2 apples, cored, peeled
   and diced

2 stalks celery, chopped
1/4 c. chopped walnuts
4 leaves lettuce

Blend mayonnaise and orange juice in a small bowl. Add apples, celery and walnuts; toss to coat. Arrange lettuce leaves on 4 salad plates; top with salad. Serves 4.

Marinated Broccoli Salad

2 bunches broccoli, sliced
   into flowerets
1 t. dill weed

1/2 c. olive oil
1/2 c. red wine vinegar
2 cloves garlic, minced

Place ingredients in a gallon-size plastic zipping bag; seal and shake well. Refrigerate overnight, shaking occasionally. Makes 6 to 8 servings.

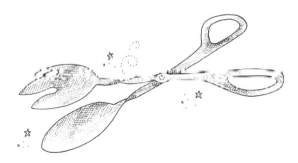

Take along a few boxed rice mixes. Serve as an easy side with grilled meats or create a hearty one-dish meal in a jiffy by stirring in leftover meat & veggies.

Hearty Vegetable Beef Soup

1 lb. ground beef
1 c. onion, chopped
3 c. water
28-oz. can diced tomatoes
2 c. potatoes, peeled
  and diced
1 c. carrots, peeled and sliced

1 c. celery, chopped
1 t. browning and
  seasoning sauce
1 t. salt
1/4 t. pepper
1 t. dried basil
1 bay leaf

Brown ground beef and onion over medium heat in a large saucepan; drain. Add remaining ingredients; heat to boiling. Reduce heat; cover and simmer for 20 minutes, until veggies are tender. Discard bay leaf. Makes 8 to 10 servings.

Invite friends to share a big pot of vegetable soup...they can bring along any veggies to add to the soup. Vegetable soup has never tasted better!

Minnesota Chicken & Wild Rice Soup

6-oz. pkg. long grain and
  wild rice, uncooked
2 c. cooked chicken, diced
2 10-3/4 oz. cans cream
  of mushroom soup
2 10-3/4 oz. cans
  cream of celery soup

14-1/2 oz. can chicken broth
Optional: 2 T. sherry
4-oz. pkg. sliced mushrooms
1 carrot, peeled
  and shredded
2 c. half-and-half

Prepare rice in a large saucepan according to package
directions. When done, stir in remaining ingredients except
half-and-half. Cook over medium heat until mushrooms are
tender. Reduce heat to low; gradually stir in half-and-half.
Simmer without boiling for about 30 minutes, stirring
frequently. Makes 6 servings.

If you enjoy creamy soups, try substituting canned
evaporated milk for half-and-half. It doesn't need
refrigeration and is lower in fat too.

Best-Ever Grilled Cheese Sandwiches

3-oz. pkg. cream cheese, softened
3/4 c. mayonnaise-type salad dressing
1 c. shredded mozzarella cheese
1 c. shredded Cheddar cheese
1/4 t. garlic powder
1/8 t. seasoned salt
10 slices bread
2 T. butter, softened

Blend cream cheese and salad dressing until smooth; stir in cheeses, garlic powder and salt. Spread half the bread slices with cheese mixture. Top with remaining bread; butter outer sides of sandwiches. Grill in a skillet over medium heat until golden on both sides. Makes 5 sandwiches.

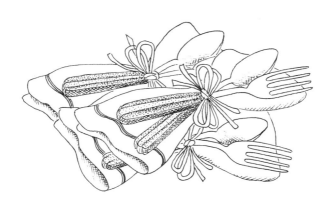

Non-slip shelf liner is oh-so handy for keeping kitchen supplies from sliding around...just cut to size and place in cupboards and drawers. Put pieces of shelf liner between pots & pans too...no more rattling!

Creamy Tomato Soup

28-oz. can diced tomatoes,
    plain or with basil,
    garlic and oregano
1 c. chicken broth
1/4 c. butter

2 T. sugar
2 T. onion, chopped
1/8 t. baking soda
2 c. whipping cream

Combine all ingredients except cream in a saucepan. Cover and simmer over low heat for 30 minutes. Warm cream separately; add to tomato mixture just before serving. Serves 6 to 8.

California Corn & Avocado Salad

16-oz. pkg. frozen
    corn, thawed
1 tomato, diced
2 T. lime juice
1 T. olive oil

1 t. dried cilantro
1/4 t. salt
1/4 t. sugar
1 avocado, diced

Combine all ingredients except avocado; mix well. Fold in avocado; cover and chill. Serves 4.

Fit a whole spice rack into a small space...just fill mini plastic zipping bags with favorite spices & seasonings. Remember to label them with a permanent marker!

Yummy Tuna Spread

2 6-oz. cans tuna, drained
8-oz. pkg. light cream cheese
1/2 c. light mayonnaise
2 T. onion, minced
1 t. dried parsley

1/2 t. hot pepper sauce
1/2 t. pepper
1 t. dried parsley
1/2 t. dried chives
hard rolls or crackers

In a small mixing bowl, blend all ingredients except rolls or crackers with a hand mixer; chill. Serve as a sandwich spread on hard rolls or as an appetizer spread with crackers. Makes about 3 cups.

Cape Cod Clam Chowder

3 potatoes, peeled and diced
2 10-3/4 oz. cans New
    England clam chowder
10-3/4 oz. can cream
    of celery soup

10-3/4 oz. can cream
    of potato soup
2 pts. half-and-half
salt and pepper to taste
Garnish: saltine crackers

In a large stockpot, boil potatoes in water for about 10 minutes until tender; drain. Add soups and half-and-half; place over medium-low heat until heated through, stirring often. Add salt and pepper to taste. Serve with crackers. Serves 6 to 8.

Good company in a
journey makes the
way seem shorter.

—Izaak Walton

Tom Turkey Club Sandwiches

6 slices bread, toasted
1/4 c. mayonnaise
8 thin slices deli turkey

1 tomato, thinly sliced
6 slices bacon, crisply cooked
Garnish: sweet pickles

Spread toasted bread slices on one side with mayonnaise; arrange turkey on 2 slices. Top turkey with 2 slices toast, mayo-side up. Add tomato and bacon; top with last 2 slices toast, mayo-side down. Cut each sandwich diagonally into 4 triangles. Garnish with sweet pickles. Makes 2 sandwiches.

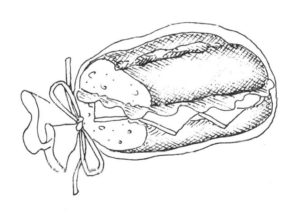

Pack some cheese cubes, multi-grain crackers, nuts and dried fruits...you'll be prepared to enjoy an instant meal at stops in scenic yet out-of-the-way locations.

Mom's One-Pot Pork Chop Dinner

1 T. butter
4 pork chops
3 potatoes, peeled and sliced
2 c. baby carrots or
    green beans

1 onion, sliced
10-3/4 oz. can cream
    of mushroom soup
1/4 c. water

Melt butter in a skillet over medium heat. Brown pork chops
for 3 to 5 minutes on each side. Add vegetables to skillet.
Combine soup and water; pour over chops and vegetables.
Cover and simmer for 15 to 20 minutes, or until chops are
done and vegetables are tender. Makes 4 servings.

Picnic Pineapple Gelatin

20-oz. can pineapple slices
3-oz. pkg. favorite-flavor
    gelatin mix

1 c. boiling water
Garnish: lettuce leaves

Drain pineapple, leaving slices in the can. Dissolve gelatin in
boiling water; pour into the can over the pineapple. Chill for
2-1/2 hours or overnight, until set. To serve, run a knife
around inside of can and slide out gelatin. Slice between
pineapple slices; arrange on lettuce leaves. Serves 5 to 6.

*One-pot meals are perfect for the RV way of life...less
fuss, less muss and more time to enjoy chatting with new
friends, sightseeing and just relaxing!*

Hobo Dinner

1-1/2 lbs. ground beef
1 t. Worcestershire sauce
1/2 t. seasoned pepper
1/8 t. garlic powder
3 redskin potatoes, sliced

1 onion, sliced
3 carrots, peeled and halved
olive oil and dried parsley
   to taste

Combine ground beef, Worcestershire sauce and seasonings;
form into 4 to 6 patties. Place each patty on an 18-inch length
of heavy-duty aluminum foil; arrange vegetables evenly on
top of patties. Sprinkle with olive oil and parsley to taste.
Wrap tightly in aluminum foil; arrange packages on a baking
sheet. Bake at 375 degrees for one hour. Packages may also
be grilled over hot coals for 30 to 35 minutes, turning 3 or
4 times. Makes 4 to 6 servings.

A Hobo Dinner is so tasty and so versatile! Substitute
pork chops, bratwurst or cut-up chicken for ground beef
patties...add peppers, squash, or even corn on the cob.
Mouthwatering!

One-Pot Spaghetti

1 lb. ground beef
1 onion, diced
2 14-oz. cans chicken broth
6-oz. can tomato paste
1/2 t. dried oregano
1/2 t. salt

1/4 t. pepper
1/8 t. garlic powder
8-oz. pkg. spaghetti,
  uncooked
Garnish: grated Parmesan
  cheese

Brown ground beef and onion in a large skillet over medium heat. Drain; return to skillet. Stir in broth, tomato paste and seasonings; bring to a boil. Break spaghetti into short lengths and add to skillet. Reduce heat and simmer, stirring often, for 15 minutes, or until spaghetti is tender. Sprinkle with cheese. Makes 4 servings.

Whip up tasty meals on the road in a flash, with no frying mess! Back home, brown ground beef and chopped onion. Drain, then pack one-pound portions in flat containers or plastic zipping bags for your RV's freezer.

Italian Garlic Salad

1/4 c. olive oil
1 to 2 cloves garlic, minced
3/4 t. seasoned salt
1 head iceberg lettuce, torn

1/2 c. shredded mozzarella
cheese or crumbled
Gorgonzola cheese

Whisk together oil, garlic and salt in a serving bowl. Toss with lettuce; top with cheese. Serves 4 to 6.

Green Pea Salad

4 slices bacon, crisply cooked
and crumbled
10-oz. pkg. frozen peas,
thawed
3 green onions, sliced

1 stalk celery, sliced
1/4 c. mayonnaise
1/4 c. sour cream
1/4 t. salt
1/8 t. pepper

Combine all ingredients in a serving bowl; chill. Serves 6.

Free up precious drawer space....use mini stick-on hooks
and clips to hang up potholders, tea towels, utensils and
other cooking must-haves in your RV's kitchen. Clever!

South-of-the-Border Beef & Beans

1 lb. ground beef	1/4 t. salt
1/4 c. onion, chopped	1/2 t. chili powder
15-1/2 oz. can kidney beans, drained and rinsed	1 c. shredded Cheddar cheese
10-oz. can enchilada sauce	Optional: tortilla chips

Crumble ground beef in a 2-quart microwave-safe glass dish. Stir in onion; cover and microwave on high for 6 minutes, until ground beef is browned. Drain; stir in remaining ingredients except cheese and tortilla chips. Microwave on high an additional 12 to 14 minutes; sprinkle with cheese. Let stand, covered, for 5 minutes, or until cheese melts. Garnish with tortilla chips, if desired. Serves 4 to 6.

Microwaved food continues to cook for several minutes after being removed. Let dinner stand just a few minutes...this extra time lets food finish cooking.

Chicken Cacciatore

6 boneless, skinless
   chicken breasts
28-oz. jar tomato & basil
   pasta sauce
2 green peppers, sliced

1 onion, minced
2 T. garlic, minced
4-1/2 oz. can sliced
   mushrooms, drained
prepared spaghetti or rice

Place chicken in a slow cooker; top with remaining ingredients
except spaghetti or rice. Cover and cook on low setting for
7 to 9 hours. Serve over prepared spaghetti or rice. Serves 6.

A slow cooker cooks up melt-in-your-mouth meats and
simmering soups with almost no work! On the road,
set the slow cooker in the sink...it won't slide off the
kitchen counter.

Ham & Broccoli Baked Potatoes

2 baking potatoes
1/2 c. cooked ham, diced
1/2 c. broccoli, cooked
   and chopped

2 slices American cheese
2 t. green onion, chopped

Pierce potatoes with a fork; microwave on high until tender,
6 to 8 minutes. Slice lengthwise and crosswise; squeeze open.
Top each potato with 1/4 cup each ham and broccoli. Arrange
a cheese slice on each. Microwave an additional minute, or
until cheese is melted. Sprinkle with green onion. Serves 2.

Traveling with children? Give 'em each their own road
map...they can trace the route with markers and see how
much farther there is to go.

Skillet Honey Chicken

2 T. butter   1/2 c. orange juice
2 T. honey
4 to 6 boneless, skinless
   chicken breasts

In a large skillet, melt butter with honey over medium heat.
Add chicken and brown on both sides. Reduce heat; continue
cooking until juices run clear when chicken is pierced. Reduce
heat to low. Drizzle with orange juice; cover and cook an
additional 10 minutes. Uncover and continue cooking until
pan juices reduce to a glaze. Serves 4 to 6.

Family Reunion Fruit Salad

20-oz. can crushed pineapple   3 oz. pkg. instant vanilla
15-oz. can fruit cocktail   pudding mix
15-oz. can mandarin oranges

Drain fruits, reserving syrup. Add pudding mix to drained fruits
and stir well. Add enough of reserved syrup to moisten to
desired consistency; chill. Makes 6 servings.

A set of unbreakable nesting bowls is oh-so handy for
mixing and serving, plus they take less storage space!

Chinatown Beef & Noodles

1-1/4 lbs. ground beef
2 3-oz. pkgs. Oriental-
   flavored ramen noodles,
   crushed, with
   seasoning packets

2 c. frozen stir-fry Oriental-
   blend vegetables, thawed
2 c. water
2 T. green onion, sliced

Brown ground beef in a large skillet; drain. Stir in one
seasoning packet; remove beef from skillet. Add noodles,
remaining seasoning packet, vegetables and water to skillet.
bring to a boil; reduce heat to medium. Cover and simmer
for 3 minutes, or until noodles are tender, stirring occasionally.
Return browned beef to skillet; heat through. Stir in green
onion and mix well. Serves 4 to 6.

Ramen noodles are a great choice for RV meals...unlike
regular pasta, they cook up quickly in just a small amount
of liquid.

Company Beef Burgundy

2 lbs. stew beef, cubed
10-3/4 oz. can cream
   of mushroom soup
8-oz. can sliced
   mushrooms, drained

3/4 c. red wine or beef broth
1-1/2 oz. pkg. onion
   soup mix
prepared noodles or rice

Combine beef, soup, mushrooms, wine or broth and soup
mix in a slow cooker. Cover and cook on low setting for
8 to 10 hours. Serve over prepared noodles or rice. Makes
4 to 6 servings.

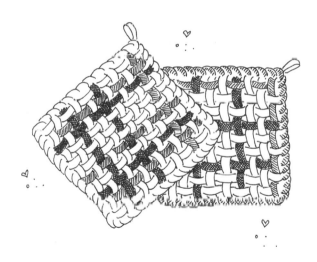

A vacuum bag sealer is useful in RV cooking. At home, use
it to prep foods that are easily stored in the fridge or
freezer. Seal and save leftovers along the way...they'll
stay extra fresh & tasty for another meal.

Spanish Rice

3 T. olive oil
1 c. long-cooking rice,
    uncooked
2 to 3 cloves garlic, minced
1/2 c. red onion, chopped

1/4 c. green pepper, chopped
14-1/2 oz. can tomatoes
    with chiles
1/2 c. chicken broth
1 T. dried cilantro

Place oil in a skillet over medium heat. Add rice; cook and stir until golden. Add garlic and sauté for one minute. Mix in onion, green pepper, undrained tomatoes and broth; bring to a boil. Reduce heat; cover and simmer until rice is done, about 15 minutes. Stir in cilantro during last few minutes of cooking. Serves 6.

White Bean &
Tomato Salad
15 oz. can cannellini or
navy beans, drained
and rinsed
3 T. olive oil
2 T lemon juice
1/4 c. fresh cilantro

Leave bulky cookbooks at home! Jot down favorite recipes for the road on 4x6-inch index cards...they'll fit perfectly into a mini flip photo album.

Zesty Macaroni & Cheese

16-oz. pkg. elbow macaroni, cooked
16-oz. pkg. pasteurized process cheese spread, cubed
8-oz. pkg. Pepper Jack cheese, cubed
2 10-3/4 oz. cans Cheddar cheese soup
1 c. onion, minced

Combine cooked macaroni and cheeses in a slow cooker. Stir in soup until everything is coated; add onion. Cover and cook on low setting for 5 to 6 hours, or on high setting for 2 hours. Stir occasionally. Makes 6 to 8 servings.

Mozzarella & Ripe Tomato Salad

8 tomatoes, chopped
1/2 c. olive oil
pepper to taste
16-oz. pkg. shredded mozzarella cheese
10 sprigs fresh basil, torn

Combine all ingredients in a large serving bowl; toss to coat. Chill for 30 minutes before serving. Makes 8 servings.

Be sure to stop at road-side stands for farm-fresh local fruits & vegetables...one of the greatest joys of traveling! You'll also find yummy baked goods, jams & jellies that you'd never get to try back home.

★ Classics ★

Triple Chocolate Delight

18-1/2 oz. pkg. chocolate
  cake mix
3.9-oz. pkg. instant
  chocolate pudding mix
16-oz. container sour cream
1 c. water

1/2 c. oil
4 eggs, beaten
6-oz. pkg. semi-sweet
  chocolate chips
Optional: frozen whipped
  topping, thawed

Combine all ingredients except whipped topping and mix well.
Pour into a greased slow cooker. Cover and cook on low setting
for 6 to 8 hours. Serve warm, topped with whipped topping if
desired. Makes 8 to 10 servings.

Quick Chocolate Cookies

9-oz. pkg. chocolate
  cake mix
1 egg

2 T. water
1 T. shortening, melted
1/2 c. chopped nuts

Blend ingredients well; drop by teaspoonfuls onto ungreased
baking sheets. Bake at 350 degrees for 10 minutes.
Makes 2 dozen.

Learning to bake in your RV's
convection oven? Here's a
guideline...cookies, bread and
pizza will all bake up as nicely as in
a regular oven, cakes and
cheesecakes won't.